THE

Servant Leader's Devotional

21-Days of Reviving Your Spirit & Leadership

T. NICOLE ALLEN

Extreme Overflow Publishing
Dacula, GA
USA

Extreme Overflow Publishing
Dacula, GA
USA

Extreme Overflow Publishing
A Brand of Extreme Overflow Enterprises, Inc
P.O. Box 1811
Dacula, GA 30019
www.extremeoverflow.com

Send feedback to info@extremeoverflow.com

Printed in the United States of America
Library of Congress Catalogin-Publication
Data is available for this title. ISBN: 978-1-7379262-2-1

THE

Servant Leader's Devotional

21-Days of Reviving Your Spirit & Leadership

T. NICOLE ALLEN

Introduction

In Luke 6:12-16, Jesus chose the original apostles, who are also known as His 12 disciples.

12 Now it came to pass in those days that He went out to the mountain to pray and continued all night in prayer to God. 13 And when it was day, He called His disciples to Himself; and from them He chose twelve whom He also named apostles: 14 Simon, whom He also named Peter, and Andrew his brother; James and John; Philip and Bartholomew; 15 Matthew and Thomas; James the son of Alphaeus; and Simon called the Zealot; 16 Judas the son of James; and Judas Iscariot who also became a traitor (Luke 6:12-16, NKJV).

During Jesus' earthly ministry, He performed miracles, taught the Word, and spent intimate time teaching His disciples how to be His servant-leaders. The New Testament Scriptures are proof of how the 12 apostles made full proof of their ministry with a made up mind to serve as unto the Lord and spread the Gospel of Jesus Christ. We find in the Scriptures various accounts of the disciples having ups and downs. Peter is one that many commonly speak of because of his impulsiveness and how his life changed forever after the resurrection of Christ, and the Day of Pentecost; when he preached a Jesus-Message so powerful that 3,000 souls were saved (Acts 2).

With this in mind, this devotional book is for the servant-leader; the five-fold ministry (Ephesians 4). Certainly, the Word of God is for everyone, and it is an absolute joy of mine to serve the Body; however, I wanted to give something special and specific to the servant-leader. Why "servant-leader?" While every leader serves, not every servant is a leader. Furthermore, not every leader is the servant-leader they ought to be. So, using the term "servant-leader" in this book is how we identify those of the five-fold ministry; those who equip and build up disciples in Christendom.

*[11] And he gave some, apostles; and some, prophets; and some, evangelists; and some, pastors and teachers; [12] **For the perfecting of the saints, for the work of the ministry, for the ed-***

ifying of the body of Christ: [13] *Till we all come in the unity of the faith, and of the knowledge of the Son of God, unto a perfect man, unto the measure of the stature of the fullness of Christ:* [14] *That we henceforth be no more children, tossed to and fro, and carried about with every wind of doctrine, by the sleight of men, and cunning craftiness, whereby they lie in wait to deceive;* [15] *But speaking the truth in love, may grow up into him in all things, which is the head, even Christ:* [16] *From whom the whole body fitly joined together and compacted by that which every joint supplieth, according to the effectual working in the measure of every part, maketh increase of the body unto the edifying of itself in love (Ephesians 4:11-16, KJV).*

With all the responsibilities and assignments they have, I believe that servant-leaders get tired; exhausted to the point that we can subconsciously serve without recognizing how we are serving. What do I mean? We become so accustomed to our custom that we just do things by default; it is a part of who we are and what we do. You know the norm – Tuesday Bible study, Thursday rehearsal, Friday service, Saturday meeting or conference, Sunday worship service, etc. Honestly, it can sometimes look robotic. Well, servant-leader (man and woman of God), as a servant-leader, I am serving you with this 21-day devotional to refresh and revive you. To encourage you to continue to "be strong in the LORD and in the power of His might" (Ephesians 6:10), and to remind you that God is with you (Joshua 1:9; Matthew 28:20).

The reasons some are not the servant-leader God desires them to be can vary. We are unappreciated by those we serve; we are betrayed by those we serve with, and like Jesus we continue to love; even when it hurts. We don't have enough laborers in our part of the Vineyard, so we are inundated and over-exerted. And with the many changes of ministry and time, transitions can sometimes be frightening. The list of reasons is more than what I've named here, but we all know where we are and can identify what challenges we face.

While in prayer the Holy Ghost laid it on my heart to write this devotional for the five-fold ministry (the servant-leaders). This book is birthed through a 21-day fast and there is a devotional for each day; inspired by the Gospel of Luke. It is my prayer that you are not only refreshed and revived, but that you receive revelation for your next sermon, your next workshop, your next ministry series, and your next song; for your next! I pray that the Holy Ghost flame in you is fanned, and that the ru-ach (ruah) of the same Spirit breathes life on what you thought died or was dying in you; in Jesus Name.

Servant-leader, receive this book as God's blessing to you. I love you and God loves you best. Continue in His grace; He is with you.

Your Fellow Servant-Leader,

Evangelist T. Nicole Allen

Day One

"Being Full of the Holy Spirit"
Luke 4:1-13

Then Jesus, being filled with the Holy Spirit, returned from the Jordan and was led by the Spirit into the wilderness, ² being tempted for 40 days by the devil. And in those days, He ate nothing, and afterward, when they had ended, He was hungry. ³ And the devil said to Him, "If You are the Son of God, command this stone to become bread." ⁴ But Jesus answered him, saying, "It is written, 'Man shall not live by bread alone, but by every word of God.'" ⁵ Then the devil, taking Him up on a high mountain, showed Him all the kingdoms of the world in a moment of time. ⁶ And the devil said to Him, "All this authority

I will give You, and their glory; for this has been delivered to me, and I give it to whomever I wish. [7] Therefore, if You will worship before me, all will be Yours." [8] And Jesus answered and said to him, "Get behind Me, Satan! For it is written, 'You shall worship the LORD your God, and Him only you shall serve.'" [9] Then he brought Him to Jerusalem, set Him on the pinnacle of the temple, and said to Him, "If You are the Son of God, throw Yourself down from here. [10] For it is written: 'He shall give His angels charge over you, To keep you,' [11] and, 'In their hands they shall bear you up, Lest you dash your foot against a stone.'" [12] And Jesus answered and said to him, "It has been said, 'You shall not tempt the LORD your God.'" [13] Now when the devil had ended every temptation, he departed from Him until an opportune time (NKJV).

Well, it is fair to begin this with "even Jesus had to be tempted by Satan..."

While Jesus is Savior of the world, and thereby divine because He is the Son of God; He entered the earth as a human being (John 1:14; Philippians 2:6, 7) and experienced the challenges of human frailty (Hebrews 4:15). However, while He experienced challenges, He did not succumb to them. Because of His divinity, Jesus was sinless; but through His humanness, He provided us with what we need to overcome sin and other challenges or temptations. My fellow servant-leader, we must read the Bible, study the Bible, and apply the Bible to our daily living. It is so easy to get drowned out by our circumstances and simply study to preach and teach, rather than study the Word to apply it, and make sure it is practical in our lives. This is how we get drained and exhausted from serving in any capacity. Time spent in prayer, fasting, and studying the Bible should not be to present only, but to be presentable!

Remember the movie "Left Behind?" After the rapture had taken place, the pastor's character (Pastor Bruce Barnes) was in the church sitting on the base of the pulpit stand bouncing the ball; and he said, "Oh LORD. Oh, God, what a fraud I am. And everybody bought it… except You… I know Your Message. I knew Your Words. I stood right here. I preached it. And I was good. But they're gone. They're gone. And… Oh but knowing and believing are two different things." He walks off the pulpit down the church aisle saying "I'm living a lie. I'm living a lie." He turned and faced the pulpit and fell to his knees, saying "Oh' God. I am kneeling before you, right now. Asking you, GOD forgive me of my sins. I am asking You to give me one more chance to receive You… use me, LORD, please, just use me." As Pastor Bruce said this prayer, the character Ray walked in and heard it. Ray touched the kneeling pastor who was asking GOD to just use him and said "He already has. He already has," and Ray also gave his life to the LORD.

There are three points I am making here, my fellow servant-leader:

1. Don't be the one who is good at presentations, but not presentable. Don't be one of the ones who will say "LORD, I prophesied in Your Name, cast out demons in Your Name, and performed many miracles in Your Name;" only to hear the LORD respond and say, "I never knew you. Get away from me, you who practice lawlessness!" (Matthew 7:21-23, NKJV).

2. GOD always has need of you. Even when you think no one is looking or no one is listening, they are. So, you have influence. No matter what you go through in life, God chose you and every experience in your life He trusts that you will allow Him to get the glory out of them all. It's up to you on how you choose to have an impact on someone's life, whether you know they're watching or listening or not. Always live as unto the LORD.

3. Choose to be led by the Holy Spirit in all things; naturally and spiritually. Be reminded that as you tell others that the Lord cares for them and that the Holy Spirit will guide them, the Holy Spirit cares for you also and will guide you. Shun the preconceived notion that you have to always show you know everything and be everything to everyone; and all the while, neglect the power of the Holy Spirit in your life. You are a disciple of Christ just like the disciples the LORD has anointed you to equip. You are ever learning and ever depending on the Holy Spirit to be the servant-leader you are, and the servant-leader GOD intends for you to be.

Luke (4:1-13) not only shares that the devil tempted Jesus, but Luke's Gospel account also shares how the devil tempted Jesus. The chapter begins by disclosing the following four things:

1) Jesus was full of the Holy Spirit.

2) Jesus was in the wilderness.

3) Jesus was fasting for 40 days and nights.

4) The devil tried to tempt Jesus when His flesh was at its weakest.

The life of the Christian certainly is not easy, let alone the life of a Christian leader, but being full of the Holy Spirit helps us during our most trying times. It's not easy to lead the most opinionated, negative, unfaithful, uncooperative, and unteachable people. People who look for fault in the leader. People who always talk about what needs to be done in the ministry but are never participants. People who behave as "pew pastors" rather than co-laborers in the Kingdom. And should we touch on our personal lives? Dealing with family challenges, marital issues (if any), issues with our secular jobs, the desire to leave the job to serve the church and do ministry full-time, the desire to sometimes just give up and quit the ministry and the church, financial burdens, struggles in the mind and with sin (lying, unforgiveness, cussing, hatred, adultery, bitterness, jealousy, fornication, depression, oppression, demonic influences, suicidal thoughts and condition), etc. The list of problems and concerns can go on.

You see, Jesus' 40-day fast was not a diet plan. Jesus was dying to His flesh and yielding Himself to the Father's will and to the power of the Holy Spirit to subdue the flesh. None of what Jesus did was easy. The 40-day fast, overcoming the temptations of Satan, remembering the Word of God during those moments of temptation, rebuking the devil (rather than yielding to him); none of that was easy. It is easy for us to overlook the depth of what Jesus had to endure in His wilderness experience because most of us read it knowing the *end*; that Jesus overcame. The Holy Spirit is our strength during those difficult times and wilderness experiences; when we feel alone with no source or resource, or when the devil tries to kick us while we're down. Our role is to submit to GOD and resist the devil in all things (James 4:7); that's the only way we will overcome.

Of everything we read here, the most crucial take away is to **be full of the Holy Spirit.** Without the Holy Spirit, we are no match for the devil, but with the Holy Spirit we can do all things (Philippians 4:13). The Holy Spirit is Jesus' promise to us. How can you resist temptation and rebuke the devil without the Holy Spirit? You can't! It's "not by might, nor by power, but by my Spirit, says the Lord of hosts (Zechariah 4:6).

Servant-leader, ask yourself the question, "What do I need to practice to help experience more of the Holy Spirit in my ministry?

PRAYER:

LORD, GOD, refill me with Your Holy Spirit. Holy Spirit, the promised Comforter, strengthen me as You did the Messiah in the wilderness to endure hardness like a good soldier. Grant me peace and build my confidence in what is both fact and truth – that Jesus already did it, so it's already done for me. LORD…

Day Two

"The Right Response"
Luke 5:1-10

So it was, as the multitude pressed about Him to hear the word of God, that He stood by the Lake of Gennesaret, ² and saw two boats standing by the lake; but the fishermen had gone from them and were washing their nets. ³ Then He got into one of the boats, which was Simon's, and asked him to put out a little from the land. And He sat down and taught the multitudes from the boat. ⁴ When He had stopped speaking, He said to Simon, "Launch out into the deep and let down your nets for a catch." ⁵ But Simon answered and said to Him, "Master, we have toiled all night and caught nothing; nevertheless, at Your

word I will let down the net." ⁶ And when they had done this,
they caught a great number of fish, and their net was breaking.
⁷ So they signaled to their partners in the other boat to come
and help them. And they came and filled both the boats, so that
they began to sink. ⁸ When Simon Peter saw it, he fell down at
Jesus' knees, saying, "Depart from me, for I am a sinful man, O
Lord!" ⁹ For he and all who were with him were astonished at
the catch of fish which they had taken; ¹⁰ and so also were James
and John, the sons of Zebedee, who were partners with Simon.
And Jesus said to Simon, "Do not be afraid. From now on you
will catch men" (NKJV).

It is noted that Jesus taught from Peter's ship, and
when Jesus finished teaching from Peter's ship, He gave
specific instructions in Luke 5:4.

1.   Launch out into the deep, and

2.   Let down your nets for draught.

These instructions, when followed, triggered an overflow of blessings! Peter and those with him caught a
countless number of fish.

So, what do we gather here? "Obedience is better than

sacrifice" (1 Samuel 15:22) and obedience to the Word of God breeds God's blessings (Deuteronomy 28:1-2).

Peter and the other fishermen sacrificed much of their time failing to catch fish, but it was their obedience that catapulted them into a blessing they didn't have enough room to receive—they had to get others to help them take it all in.

"Nevertheless, at Thy Word I will let down the net" (Luke 5:5) is the response servant-leaders must strive for. It is not always easy to *launch out into the deep.* We become so accustomed to our norm that *new* is uncomfortable for us, so we try to either ignore it or control our transition into the new. I admit that there have been times when God was making a shift in my life that I got very uncomfortable; and while my mouth said "Yes, LORD," my actions were sometimes resistant. You see, I resisted what GOD was doing in and for me by attempting to continue my same old routines, but He was calling me to something different and better. I was so used to having my real estate office set up from both my church office and from my home that I did not want to entertain the idea of getting an actual commercial space for my company. Oh, how I ignored, not only the tugging of the Holy Spirit in my heart and the dreams He gave me, but also the prophecies that were spoken over my business that I would need a new office setting. I ignored it all.

Business slowed down. Well, that made me run to Jesus. The LORD knows how to get our attention and provoke us to seek Him. One day an office space I had looked at some years back became available again. God said to me, "Go there. Launch out. Relaunch." At that point, not only were my eyes and ears open to God, but my heart was in alignment with His will. I got my new office space, and the business blossomed. God wanted me to see that the transition was an elevation!

Is God calling you to come up a little higher or to do something different or unusual? There is a right response to His call.

How can we lead people to newness if we cannot receive it for ourselves? Drawing closer to GOD keeps us in alignment with His will and gives us clarity on His instructions when He speaks. Getting closer to God means becoming more like Him and becoming more like Him means letting go of things or even people that interfere with your personal development and progress as a Christian servant-leader. I challenge you to let go of anything that is blocking your spiritual view. I'm talking about your faith; it's "The substance of things hoped for, the evidence of things not seen... and without faith, it is impossible to please God" (Hebrews 11:1, 6). So, *launching out into the deep* requires our complete trust in God.

As a servant-leader, launching out may mean applying for a new job or position, starting your new business, taking your church or ministry through an uncharted experience inspired by the Holy Spirit during your time with Him, or even birthing a church. It could also mean taking that courtship to the next level. You may be afraid to graduate from courtship to marriage because of fear of failure, or perhaps you've already had a failed marriage, but I want to remind you of three things:

1. Perfect love casts out all fear (1 John 4:18).

2. God would not present a blessing to you and take it away from you. He is inciting you to transform so that you will be in position for possession to receive His gifts and fulfillment of His promises.

Remain in a prayerful posture, and you will not disqualify yourself from the blessing God has for you. In remaining prayerful, you will always be aligned with the will of God for your life. Don't be afraid to launch out. GOD is with you.

3. Your proper posture of communing with GOD daily keeps you alert and aware of the Holy Spirit's leading in all things.

No matter the circumstance, we must remember that Jesus is always with us when we launch into the deep. When Peter launched into the deeper part of the sea, Jesus was in the ship with him. God is with you! Every hardship and every difficult situation, He is there. When you love, trust, and call on the name of Jesus, He will always be with you. The LORD will never lead you to a place HE will not accompany you!

So, by faith, we say "Nevertheless at thy word, I will let down my net." In other words, **the right response** is "I will trust You, Lord," and "Yes, Lord!"

As a servant-leader, in what ways can you practice trusting God more in your personal life and with your ministry?

PRAYER:

LORD, forgive me for the times that I chose to sacrifice over obeying You. Forgive me for substituting obedience with sacrifice. I don't want to be the servant-leader who You will allow to serve and minister to others but cannot minister to You (Ezekiel 44:10-18)! Oh, GOD, You are my life and my lifeline, and my deepest desire is to please You. Thank you, Lord for giving me an obedient heart. I will obey Your Word. Even when I may not fully understand, I acknowledge that You are God and You are in control; so I trust You, LORD. I acknowledge that my obedience to You is not optional, and only when I obey are my sacrifices received. Through my obedience, I welcome and receive Your abundance of blessings. I yield to Your will, and I say, *Yes*, Lord. I will obey. Ever give me the strength to give You the "right response," even when it isn't easy. LORD…

Day Three

"Jesus, Lord of the Sabbath"
Luke 6:1-10

Now it happened on the second Sabbath after the first that He went through the grain fields. And His disciples plucked the heads of grain and ate them, rubbing them in their hands. ² And some of the Pharisees said to them, "Why are you doing what is not lawful to do on the Sabbath?" ³ But Jesus answering them said, "Have you not even read this, what David did when he was hungry, he and those who were with him: ⁴ how he went into the house of God, took and ate the showbread, and also gave some to those with him, which is not lawful for any but the priests to eat?" ⁵ And He said to them, *"The Son of Man is also Lord of the Sabbath." ⁶ Now it happened on another Sabbath, also, that He entered the synagogue and taught. And a man was there whose right hand was withered. ⁷ So the scribes and Pharisees watched Him closely, whether He would heal on the Sabbath, that they might find an accusation against Him. ⁸ But He knew their thoughts and said to the man who had the withered hand, "Arise and stand here." And he arose and stood. ⁹ Then Jesus said to them, "I will ask you one thing: Is it lawful on the Sabbath to do good or to do evil, to save life or to destroy?" ¹⁰ And when He had looked around at them all, He said to the man, "Stretch out your hand." And he did so, and his hand was restored as whole as the other (NKJV).*

Sabbath was typically a special time to rest from work and any type of labor.

Jesus took His example of the Sabbath to the next level. In this passage, He proves how He is Lord of the Sabbath by doing what no man could do – heal and make whole. He intentionally did this on the Sabbath as evidence of His authority. He also did this to show the true meaning of the Sabbath in action.

Sabbath is not "rest from," the Sabbath is "rest in." It

is a time to "Rest in Jesus."

When we reflect on the all-sufficient grace of God, we will see that He is concerned about us every day of the week.

There is no special day or time that we are confined to seeking God. The day and time are always right to *rest in, reflect on, and seek* God. Servant-leader, not only do you need to embrace this time of rest, but know that you are entitled to it. Resting in Jesus not only allows you respite from all that you do, for personal peace and clarity, but it refreshes you to be *re-presented* to the people you serve. Selah.

If ever you had a question about your access to Jesus at times, allow me to simply *remind* you that Him proving that He is **Lord of the Sabbath** is a reflection of HIS endless availability to you! Jesus is always available to us and is a "very present Help" (Psalm 46:1).

As a servant-leader, how are you acknowledging the Sabbath? In what ways can you practice resting in God more in your personal time as well as your ministry?

PRAYER:

Father, God, in the Name of Jesus, while I realize that the Sabbath was not created for You nor was I created for the Sabbath, but rather You created the Sabbath for me (Mark 2:27-28), I ask that You increase my desire to set aside time for myself; to regroup and rest. During this time of rest, may I also rest in You; and reflect on what You've done through and for me. Help me to be attentive to what You want me to do now and what You want me to do next. It's during this time of blessed quietness and rest in You that I gain clarity of vision. LORD...

Day Four

"Just One *WORD* from JESUS"
Luke 7:1-10

Now when He concluded all His sayings in the hearing of the people, He entered Capernaum. ² And a certain centurion's servant, who was dear to him, was sick and ready to die. ³ So when he heard about Jesus, he sent elders of the Jews to Him, pleading with Him to come and heal his servant. ⁴ And when they came to Jesus, they begged Him earnestly, saying that the one for whom He should do this was deserving, ⁵ "for he loves our nation, and has built us a synagogue." ⁶ Then Jesus went with them. And when He was already not far from the house, the centurion sent friends to Him, saying to

Him, "Lord, do not trouble Yourself, for I am not worthy that You should enter under my roof. [7] Therefore I did not even think myself worthy to come to You. But say the word, and my servant will be healed. [8] For I also am a man placed under authority, having soldiers under me. And I say to one, 'Go,' and he goes; and to another, 'Come,' and he comes; and to my servant, 'Do this,' and he does it." [9] When Jesus heard these things, He marveled at him, and turned around and said to the crowd that followed Him, "I say to you, I have not found such great faith, not even in Israel!" [10] And those who were sent, returning to the house, found the servant well who had been sick. (NKJV)

Luke chapter 7 shares four life-altering stories. One occurred by JESUS' Hand, two by His Word, and one by proof of His works – the testimony of witnesses!

Not in this order, but here are the life-altering stories in Luke 7:

1. While a widowed woman's dead adult son was being carried in his coffin, **Jesus touched** the coffin and *raised* her son to life! Just when we think the worst is final, God always steps in. His *on time* is not our *on time;* yet, His touch can change the course of our lives in an instant. What is undeni-

able in this moment is that sometimes GOD sets up situations in such a way that only He can get the glory, and no one can take credit for how He has turned things around.

2. The sinful woman with the alabaster box gave Jesus everything she had in her humility. Her worship was free of pride and fear and was intentional in honoring the Messiah. Her action is what Jesus *heard.* Her action spoke and said, "forgive me." *Jesus responded* to her action and *said,* "Thy sins are forgiven" (Luke 7:48). Just one Word from JESUS can change our lives forever; giving us a fresh start, a fresh revelation, a fresh anointing, renewed faith, life to our ministry... Just one Word from Jesus can do it or fix it; "it" being whatever "it" is you need or are faced with.

3. John the Baptist sent two of his disciples to Jesus to get a direct confirmation that Jesus is the long-awaited Messiah of Israel. Jesus' response was in directing John's disciples to the *proof* of His work. Scripture tells us that "in that same hour He cured many of their infirmities and plagues, and

of evil spirits; and unto many that were blind, He gave sight" (Luke 7:21). Jesus did these things in front of John's disciples so that they could **bear witness** with their own eyes, and so they could run and tell that! *"22 Jesus answered and said to them, "Go and tell John the things you have seen and heard: that the blind see, the lame walk, the lepers are cleansed, the deaf hear, the dead are raised, the poor have the gospel preached to them. 23 And blessed is he who is not offended because of Me"* Luke 7:22-23.

Jesus knows what we need at all times, and He knows that we sometimes need to see His Hand at work in our lives or sometimes feel His touch. As servant-leaders, we sometimes, by default, exclude ourselves of having the experience with Christ that He so often uses us to give to people – His Word, His touch, our testimony of Him. So, every now and again we receive that unexpected check in the mail, or that offering that someone gently and discreetly places in our hands – some of us in Christendom call that a "holy handshake." We may also receive an encouraging phone call that uplifts us, or that overwhelming presence of the Holy Spirit that we either cry out in worship or dance in rejoicing; and many other things He does to remind us that He is LORD, and He is there.

4. Yet, of all the accounts noted in Luke 7, to me, the most powerful is that of the Centurion Soldier. Certainly, the fact that he was Roman proves that Jesus came for all humanity and not the Jews only, but what's remarkable here is the Centurion's faith in Jesus (Luke 7:6-7). The Centurion believed that Jesus' Word alone would be sufficient to fulfill his request. The unspeakable happens when our faith meets the Lord's heart. HIS virtue is released, and miracles happen. Ask the woman with the issue of blood (Matthew 9:20-22; Mark 5:25-34; Luke 8:43-48). Jesus said of Himself "Heaven and Earth shall pass away, but My Words shall not pass away" (Matthew 24:35).

The Centurion recognized the power of Christ, that even if He did not touch someone with His hands, He can reach them with His Word. You see, Jesus is the Word (John 1:14). In fact, according to Revelation 19:13, Jesus' other name is "the Word of God." Whew! That is so powerful. JESUS' Name is The Word of GOD. Remember what the Gospel of John stated, "… and the Word became flesh…" referencing JESUS? The more we hold fast to His Word, the more we're holding onto Him and are being held by Him—JESUS.

Servant-leaders, we know that the best way to know Jesus is by reading and studying the Bible. As much as we "know" this, sometimes in ministry we need simple reminders of the importance and value of the Word of GOD, and the effect it can have in our lives and those we influence.

JESUS' Words are our constant reminder that we are healed, we are whole, we are saved, we are delivered, we are free of the bondages of (all) sin, the bondages of weight (Hebrews 12:1), depression, oppression, scandals, slandering, broken relationships, and everything contrary to the will and Word of GOD. Just one Word from Jesus will alter and change the trajectory of your ministry and your life forever! **Just one Word from JESUS…**

My fellow servant-leader, in what ways can you practice trusting that "one Word" from God for your life and ministry; no matter what obstacles you are faced with?

PRAYER:

LORD, forgive me for the times that I neglected Your Word, did not spend enough time in Your Word, acted contrary to Your Word, did not believe Your Word, or behaved as though I did not believe or trust Your Word, did not share Your Word, and/or did not hide Your Word in my heart as I ought. Remind me of Your Word. Yes, LORD. Holy Spirit, I set aside all distractions and hindrances that would block my senses from You. So, You are welcome to bring the Word back to my remembrance. Today, as I remember the lyrics of the late Andrae Crouch, "always remember JESUS, JESUS… always keep Him on your mind;" may I be reminded, JESUS, that You are the Word, and they that keep their mind stayed on the WORD (JESUS), You shall keep them in perfect peace. I realize, LORD, that the way I treat my Bible is the way I am treating You because You are the Word. I value You, GOD; more than anything.

I pray, dear LORD, that no matter the circumstances, be it good or bad, may I ever remember to ask myself "What did GOD say?" I know that in that moment, my heart, eyes, and ears will be open to You, and I will be reminded of Your Word. GOD, in the beginning, You said, "let there be, and it was... and it was good" (Genesis 1). You have given me creative power to speak Your Word and call things into existence and alignment according to Your Word and will because "Death and life are in the power of the tongue: and they that love it shall eat the fruit thereof" (Proverbs 18:21). I choose to speak what JESUS gave, "life." LORD, I choose to...

Day Five

"Keep Going, Don't Quit"
Luke 8:22-25

Now it happened, on a certain day, that He got into a boat with His disciples. And He said to them, "Let us cross over to the other side of the lake." And they launched out. ²³ But as they sailed, He fell asleep. And a windstorm came down on the lake, and they were filling with water, and were in jeopardy. ²⁴ And they came to Him and awoke Him, saying, "Master, Master, we are perishing!" Then He arose and rebuked the wind and the raging of the water. And they ceased, and there was a calm. ²⁵ But He said to them, "Where is your faith?" And they were afraid, and marveled, saying to one another, "Who can this be? For He commands even the winds and water, and they obey Him!" (NKJV)

Luke 8:22-25 shares that Jesus entered a ship with His disciples and tells them "let us go over to the other side." What the disciples did not foresee was the great storm that would come to frighten them and make them think they would die in the storm. You see, that's what fear does, it grips you to the degree that you feel paralyzed and cannot move. In fact, fear will make you feel anxious and cause you to panic. Of his many tactics, here are two things out of many that **Satan** is attempting to do with his fear-tactics:

1. He is trying to stop you from doing the will of GOD which both blocks the expansion of the Kingdom of God and the blessings that come with being obedient to the Word of God. Just because trouble comes and often, servant-leaders, it is greater than we anticipated, it is still not an excuse to abort the assignment. Do not abort. You are just on the brink of something great, so go through the storm understanding that you are not going through alone. If JESUS can rest in your storm, certainly you can too!

2. He is trying to overwork your mind and emotions to the degree that you will self-sabotage and destroy what is on the other side of the storm for you. If you panic in a storm, you are not at peace, which means you cannot hear GOD amid the chaos of your trouble. In moments of anxiety and perplexity be reminded of the following three things:

- "God is not the author of confusion, but of peace..." (1 Corinthians 14:33). Confusion is chaotic and is contrary to the character of GOD, who brings order to disorder.

- "In the beginning... the earth was without form and void; and darkness was on the face of the deep... Then God said, 'Let there be light' and there was light. And God saw the light, that was good; and God divided the light from darkness" (Genesis 1:2-4). The enemy would have you focus on the darkness (dreariness) of your situation which ultimately dims the light in you. You must remember that you are like a city that cannot be hid, and dark moments are opportunities to shine bright. Shine bright, servant-leader; shine bright (Matthew 5:14).

- "From the ends of the earth I will cry out (call) to You when my heart is overwhelmed (faint); lead me to the rock that is higher than I" (Psalm 61:2). Storms are not only tumultuous, but they are equally draining, causing heaviness and exhaustion. Heaviness not only makes us tired, but it can weigh down our praise if we allow it; this is why we ask God to take us to a place of security in Him that our troubles are overcome by His mercy, grace, and love. Servant-leader, you have access to God, whom you preach and teach others about; use it!

Oftentimes as servant-leaders, when God is moving us to something more, we are faced with conflict we did not foresee and want to give up. Many of us realize that every time God is getting ready to bless us even more, the devil makes attempts to block us from believing, seeing, and receiving the blessing. Jesus was fast asleep on the ship when a great windstorm came and filled the ship with water, as to sink it, but Jesus "rebuked both the wind and the raging of water and they ceased, and there was a calm" (Luke 8:24).

We must trust God and believe that He will not allow the heavy winds of life and the raging waters in our lives to throw us into a place that we cannot recover from or drown us in. God allows the storms in our lives so we can:

1. See our desperate need for him. We cannot get through life and ministry without Jesus being the Head of our life, and

2. Build our faith in Him. Jesus is not only with us, but He is within us (Romans 10:9). You are not in that violent wind or raging water by yourself. The Lord is with(in) you. Only believe. Jesus asked, "where is your faith?" (Luke 8:25). You must **trust** that the Lord is with you and believe that He will not let any storm take you out.

The purpose and plan He has for your life and ministry is far greater than the storms you face and the storms that will come. Yes, my fellow servant-leader, you already know that there are more storms to come, which means more storms to overcome. **So, keep going. Don't quit.**

Expect challenges when you are growing and making progress; expect the devil to try to thwart the plan of God for your life and ministry. Most importantly, expect God to be with you and bring you out of the storm because He has you covered; and He cares. Expect victory.

As a servant-leader, what Scriptures are most comforting and reassuring for your life and ministry when storms arise?

PRAYER:

Dear LORD, today I pray that when things get turbulent in my life and ministry that You endow me, in abundance, with peace, strength, and joy. I desire Your peace because I know it will keep me from anxiety and depression. I desire Your strength because it helps me to "endure hardness like a good soldier;" and Your joy because it is both my strength and the reason for my praise. May I ever have the joy of Thy salvation, Oh Lord, as You continue to "uphold me with Your free Spirit." GOD, You are faithful, and I respond to Your faithfulness by being faithful to You; the One who calms the storms in my life, so that I can continue, steadfastly, in my God-given assignment(s). Let my life please You, LORD...

Day Six

"Live to Tell the Story"
Luke 8:39

R*eturn to your own house, and tell what great things God has done for you." And he went his way and proclaimed throughout the whole city what great things Jesus had done for him.*
(NKJV)

Luke 8:26-39 tells of how Jesus delivered a demon-possessed man from many demons named "Legion." This demonic-possession had the man harming himself and breaking the chains he was bound in, only to be driven into the wilderness. This demon-possessed man didn't live in a house, but he "abode" in tombs (Luke 8:27). As we all know, tombs are where the dead lay.

How detrimental was the tragedy of your life that you decided to give up on yourself and wallow in that dead, yet tormenting, situation? So often some people look at Christian leaders as though they cannot go through heartrending experiences that would make them want to just stop; stop serving, stop working, stop praying, stop loving, stop living, and stop so many other things. Some leaders have actually stopped; stopped in their Christian walk and apostatize from the Christian Faith. Some are preaching, but stopped reaching people. Singing, but stopped praising. Giving, but stopped receiving love and healing.

You see, that sickness, that betrayal, that scandal, the broken marriage, the lost job, missed opportunities, sickness, loss of a loved one that you didn't reconcile with before their death, and so many more unsaid disappointments or struggles are all things that could make someone want to run into a cave and hide forever if you could. It could make you ashamed, bitter, distrusting, and unforgiving, but GOD doesn't stop reeling us back in.

Luke 8:22 says "Let us go over to the other side of the lake..." So, we should consider that:

1. Jesus came to the other side just to deliver this demon-possessed man from his torment. Isn't that like God? It is just like God to come to the rescue to deliver us from the painful trauma of our past and present situations. God will come through just for you.

2. Jesus showed His disciples that sometimes we have to go the extra mile or above and beyond for people who don't realize that GOD sent you to be a help to them.

3. Jesus, without hesitation, gives of His anointing and time. Understand that...

   • The reward from the Father is greater than what we can give.

   • Jesus intentionally took time to retreat, rest, be refreshed, and refilled so He could do it all again. This is the cycle of ministry, servant-leaders. We allow the LORD to fill us up as His vessels and then empty us as we pour out to His people; however, He sees fit to use us in any assignment, and then we go home (or on vacation) to retreat, rest, be refreshed, and refilled so we can continue to be the laborers in the Vineyard He has called us to be (not just within the church walls, but outside. The Church is without borders)!

The humiliations and tragedies God brought you out of are not meant to be closeted but to (1) help others; and (2) to allow those who thought you'd crumble and die in the tomb of shame to witness you with peace and joy and acknowledge that it had to be God (Luke 8:35). Don't hide and don't stop, but stand and live. Live to serve. **Live to tell the story,** servant-leader.

As a servant-leader, in what ways can you wisely practice transparency more in your life and ministry?

PRAYER:

Father, GOD, in the Name of JESUS. Forgive me for hiding from my past and present issues rather than hiding behind the Cross that makes my witness all about you and less about me. While the things or situations You have delivered me from certainly involve me, the deliverance and testimony is about You and Your grace. How gracious it was for You to go to "the other side" to deliver a man who was tormented by demons, while others who had no power to save, heal, and deliver would watch from afar. Thank you, LORD, for not watching me in my struggle, but delivering me from it so I can be effective in what You have assigned me to do. LORD, I choose to live to tell the story. Holy Spirit, empower me to testify with conviction, of the saving power and grace of JESUS CHRIST. LORD...

Day Seven

"Heart of a Servant"
Luke 9:43-48

And they were all amazed at the majesty of God. But while everyone marveled at all the things which Jesus did, He said to His disciples, ^{44} "Let these words sink down into your ears, for the Son of Man is about to be betrayed into the hands of men." ^{45} But they did not understand this saying, and it was hidden from them so that they did not perceive it; and they were afraid to ask Him about this saying. ^{46} Then a dispute arose among them as to which of them would be greatest. ^{47} **And Jesus, perceiving the thought of their heart, took a little child and set him by Him,** ^{48} and said to them, "Whoever *receives this little child in My name receives Me; and whoever receives Me receives Him who sent Me. For he who is least among you all will be great" (NKJV).*

Jesus' disciples, like others who witnessed His wonder-working power, were amazed by Him. They were amazed by what He could do. After casting the devil out of a child (Luke 9:38-42), Jesus told His disciples to truly listen to Him as He disclosed to them His impending suffering. While they didn't understand, they did not ask for understanding; rather their ambition was misdirected by wanting to know who would be greatest among them.

Our focus should not be on our own greatness or on how we can or will be greater than the next ministry or conference. Our focus should not be on why church members are so unfaithful and inconsistent. We ask questions like "What is wrong with these people?" "Why won't they come to church?" "Why won't they participate in worship?" "Why won't the praise team learn new songs?" "Why don't this…" and "Why don't that…?" Valid questions but still the wrong questions. It should be "LORD, what do You want me to do today?" "Where do You want me to go today?" "Who do You want me to bless today?" "Give me strategy on how to evangelize today," or "Help me to disciple Your people effectively." Our focus should always be on our great God and His will, which has been the Great Commission since around A.D. 29–30. Although time and strategies change, the Lord's charge to us has not. As we turn our hearts towards Jesus, great things happen for us (Matthew 6:33).

It is from the heart that the mouth speaks (Luke 6:45). Jesus, while He was not in the disciples' conversation, knew their heart (Luke 9:47). Jesus used the example of a child to express the level of humility we should have as disciples and servants. Greatness is not based on our status, labor, looks, or even on who we know. It is based on humility. Humility does not seek greatness. Humility seeks the Great One; JESUS!

Servant-leaders, as we channel (or re-channel) our focus on God, with a **heart of a servant,** His plan will unfold in our lives.

As a servant-leader, in what ways can you practice humility more in your life and ministry?

PRAYER:

GOD, forgive me for being so focused on me, my accomplishments or lack thereof, and not setting my "affections on things above" as I should. I know that as I serve You, Your plan for my life is fulfilled, but sometimes I get in my own way. Help me redirect my heart and focus on You. LORD, sometimes, I even convince myself because I am Your servant, what I am doing is Your will; but LORD, I'm sorry for the times I've missed. I come clean before You, and I admit that I have missed the mark, concerning myself, my family, and even my ministry. Yet, LORD, GOD, "Thou knowest all things," so I thank You for these moments that remind me of how much I need You, and how I cannot do anything without You. LORD, JESUS, I don't want to try to make it without You, and I don't want to embark on greatness if it is not a door or window You've opened or a way You've made. LORD...

Day Eight

"There Are Others"
Luke 10:1

After these things the Lord appointed seventy others also and sent them two by two before His face into every city and place where He Himself was about to go (NKJV).

You ever have a day where your agenda was so full that when the day ended, you crashed across your bed or on your sofa? Just burnt out from doing your best? Burnt out from life? From sermon preparation to delivery of the sermon, from conference to conference, workshops, outings, counseling, mentorship, church programs, hospital visits, prison visits, and so much more that entails the responsibilities of servant-leaders. Well, I certainly have experienced being burnt out, and while our days can undoubtedly be full, we must be sure they are not full because the load was not shared. The question we must ask ourselves is "Could I have gotten help? And Who could help?"

As leaders, we often don't solicit help for the following reasons:

1. We feel we can do what needs to be done before having to explain it.

2. We feel we'll do it better because we know how we want things done.

3. We don't think who we ask can actually do the job or would be willing to do what needs to be done.

What does that say about us in our apprehension to delegate? It tells us that we need to work on our trust, patience, self-righteousness, worries (anxiety), and being judgmental (Matthew 7:1-5). We must recognize our imperfections and then have gratitude that the Lord still chose to give us an agenda.

Have you ever considered that God allowed your schedule to be full so that you could share your load with someone else? Perhaps you have so much or enough work to solicit the help of more than one person and delegate responsibility. I'll go a step further to say that God may have allowed you to have so much to do so that you can help others learn how to do! Yes! Remember, our lives are not about us. As a servant-leaders, it is always about the Lord and our serving Him.

Other versions of the Bible, such as the NIV and NLT, state that Jesus appointed "72" disciples in Luke 10:1. However, according to Luke 10:1 (NKJV), Jesus appointed 70 disciples. The point is not about if it were 70 or 72, but the fact is that Jesus called more disciples outside of the 12 who were His direct company. He charged the 70 (or 72) to do the work He also charged His 12 disciples to do (Luke 9:1-2). The 70 (or 72) that Jesus appointed came back with a good report and said to Jesus "Lord, even the demons obey us when we use Your Name!" (Luke 10:17, NIV). You would be amazed at what those who do not appear to be in the "inner-circle" can accomplish just by knowing who they are in Christ, knowing their assignment from Him, and fulfilling it.

Today we are reminded of three things:

1. We are never alone - Jesus is always with us. **There are others** who feel like we do, and the Lord is with them too.

2. We are not the only ones—**there are others** who the Lord has called and chosen. So, we must remain humble and prepared to equip others, not deprive them of the growth and knowledge they need to be effective disciples.

3. It is not about us. The moment we seek GOD's will and agenda, we get strategy for our day-to-day to-do list. Remember, **there are others** who need our direction on how to navigate through the "woe is me" syndrome that we can easily get ensnared with if we lose focus.

As a servant-leader, in what ways can you practice equipping help and delegating more in your ministry and in your personal life?

PRAYER:

Holy Spirit, fill me, teach me, guide me, and remind me that in everything I do, I must do it as unto the Lord; and that includes your compassion and love. LORD, JESUS, through Your compassion let Your patience be heightened in me; and through Your love, let Your grace abound through me. Yes, "…When my heart is overwhelmed, lead me to the rock that is higher than I," (Psalm 61:2); yet may I ever be mindful that Your Kingdom was expanded because of the fellowship and sharing of believers (Acts 2:44). Thank you, Holy Spirit, for reminding me that there are others who love You, others who seek You, others who are tried for Your cause, others who live for You, and others who desire to learn more about how to serve You. I ask You, in the Name of Jesus, to help me, strengthen me, and anoint me to share what You have given me with others…

Day Nine

"Acknowlegment in Prayer"
Luke 11:1-13

Now it came to pass, as He was praying in a certain place, when He ceased, that one of His disciples said to Him, "Lord, teach us to pray, as John also taught his disciples." [2] So He said to them, "When you pray, say: Our Father in heaven, Hallowed be Your name. Your kingdom come. Your will be done on earth as it is in heaven. [3] Give us day by day our daily bread. [4] And forgive us our sins, For we also forgive everyone who is indebted to us. And do not lead us into temptation but deliver us from the evil one." [5] And He said to them, "Which of you shall have a friend, and go to him at midnight and say to him, 'Friend, lend me three loaves; [6] for a friend of mine has come to me on his journey, and I have nothing to set before him;' [7] and he will answer from within and say, 'Do not trouble me; the door is now shut, and my children are with me in bed; I cannot rise and give to you?' [8] I say to you, though he will not rise and give to him because he is his friend, yet because of his persistence he will rise and give him as many as he needs. [9] "So I say to you, ask, and it will be given to you; seek, and you will find; knock, and it will be opened to you. [10] For everyone who asks receives, and he who seeks finds, and to him who knocks it will be opened. [11] If a son asks for bread from any father among you, will he give him a stone? Or if he asks for a fish, will he give him a serpent instead of a fish? [12] Or if he asks for an egg, will he offer him a scorpion? [13] If you then, being evil, know how to give good gifts to your children, how much more will your heavenly Father give the Holy Spirit to those who ask Him!" (NKJV).

"Father God in the Name of Jesus, forgive me; please do this; please do that; Lord, you know... and God make a way; have Your way; turn it around. Save, deliver, and set free..." We say all of this and more when we talk to God.

While most times, if not always, we know and are

confident that GOD hears us when we pray; sometimes there are gentle reminders that GOD is not looking for complex prayers, just a humble and sincere heart. I admit, there were times that I placed more of a demand on myself about how to pray than GOD did; and those self-demands only caused me to slack in my prayer life. However, one morning, during my time with the Lord, I was reminded by the Holy Spirit that all GOD wants is acknowledgement. The author of Hebrews said it so simple, yet so direct, "… for he that comes to GOD must believe that He is, and that He is a rewarder of those who diligently seek Him" (Hebrews 11:6).

Don't get so drowned out by the routine of praying for others, whether publicly or privately, that you forget that GOD is concerned about you and hears you, too. We need to do just as we teach, preach, and admonish others to do – simply be ourselves and be confident that Our Father Who is in Heaven hears us, will answer us, help us, protect us, provide for us, deliver us, and strengthen us… HE will respond to us when we call. In fact, the LORD answers us before we call Him. Isaiah 65:24 states, "Before they call, I will answer; while they are still speaking, I will hear."

Despite what they witnessed of JESUS; the disciples wanted to know more about Him. I imagine they watched Him pray often, and it is impossible to be in the LORD'S presence and not desire to model His example; to be like Him.

Servant-leaders, it is okay to ask the LORD to guide us in prayer. I had some life experiences that certainly threw me some curve balls and made praying difficult, but it did not make prayer less essential. Truthfully, it made prayer more necessary than ever for me, but it was so hard. So, I asked the LORD to teach me again. I said "Holy Spirit, guide me in prayer. Show me how to pray through this. Show me how to address the Father with this. Help me, Holy Spirit." And that's exactly what the Helper did; He helped me (John 14:26, ESV, NKJV).

In Luke 11, Jesus' disciples ask for a lesson on how to pray. Jesus' instructions for prayer are a simple and powerful outline to ensure our prayers are heard, and that we can go further (deeper) in our time of prayer when we recognize Him and make the outline He has provided practical. Jesus simply states in "The Lord's Prayer" the following:

1. **Acknowledge** God, His pre-existence, and His holiness.

2. **Acknowledge** His kingdom and for His Kingdom-will, to be done on earth; and submit yourself to that (His will).

3. **Acknowledge** that everything you need, and desire comes only through Him. He is not only the Divine source. He is the only Source for all things.

4. **Praying the Word.** The Word is crucial to the Christian's daily life and is what God responds to. The psalmist said to the Lord, "Remember the Word to Your servant, upon which You have caused me to hope. This is my comfort in my affliction, for Your Word has given me life" (Psalm 119:49-50, NKJV).

5. **Ask Him to forgive you** for all things that displease Him and to help you to forgive others; especially when it is most difficult to do so. "…if you do not forgive others their sins, your Father will not forgive your sins" (Matthew 6:15, NIV).

6. **Ask Him to continue to empower you** to resist

temptation (James 4:7) and to deliver you from everything that will deter you from His will and your influence in the lives of others.

7. **Remember others** when you pray.

8. **Be persistent and consistent** in prayer (Luke 4:8).

9. **Ask the Holy Spirit** to lead, guide, and direct you.

As a servant-leader, in what ways can you show GOD your vulnerability in prayer for a deeper relationship with Christ and your family, and for every area of your life and ministry?

PRAYER:

Father, GOD, in the Name of Jesus, I acknowledge You and my desperate need for Your will to be fulfilled in my life and for those who I have, and continue to pray for. I first ask for Your forgiveness. May I never overlook Your sovereignty and providential care. I admit that just when I think forgiveness isn't an issue in my life, an offense from Satan may try to throw me off course from my prayer life, which would ultimately throw me of course from Your will. Satan tried to buffet me, but Holy Spirit, You reminded me of the Words of JESUS when HE said...

Day Ten

"Look In"
Luke 11:38-44

When the Pharisee saw it, he marveled that He had not first washed before dinner. *39 Then the Lord said to him, "Now you Pharisees make the outside of the cup and dish clean, but your inward part is full of greed and wickedness. 40 Foolish ones! Did not He who made the outside make the inside also? 41 But rather give alms of such things as you have, then indeed all things are clean to you. 42 "But woe to you Pharisees! For you tithe mint and rue and all manner of herbs and pass by justice and the love of God. These you ought to have done, without leaving the others undone. 43 Woe to you*

Pharisees! For you love the best seats in the synagogues and greetings in the marketplaces. [44] Woe to you, scribes and Pharisees, hypocrites! For you are like graves which are not seen, and the men who walk over them are not aware of them" (NKJV).

The Pharisee who invited Jesus to dine with him was taken aback by Jesus not washing His hands before sitting at the table to eat. Jesus, knowing all things, addressed this by reproving the Pharisees for being more concerned about their outward presentation than their inner transformation. This is why it's not enough to honor God with our lips, and our hearts be far from Him (Isaiah 29:13; Matthew 15:8-9). We can say the right things, look like the right thing, and even do the right thing when it comes to routines, but what is needful is to live right(eous).

Masquerading in smiles that are not incited by the joy of the Lord's salvation (Psalm 51:12). Overcompensating beauty with things (cars, clothing, jewelry, devices, etc.) and calling such masquerades "confidence in God" and "fearfully wonderfully made" (Psalm 139:14) can be a display of hidden secret struggles and sin. While we think others cannot see, God can clearly see because His eyes are in every place (Proverbs 15:3).

Servant-leaders, we cannot be so concerned about how we look outwardly or even how we are perceived outwardly that we neglect or lose sight on what needs to happen inwardly. We cannot be concerned about how we look to others, and what routines or traditions we did or did not do correctly. Remember, GOD is THE SEARCHER OF OUR HEARTS (Romans 8:27). He knows all things. Things that are hidden from others are never hidden from GOD. So, it is incumbent upon us to examine ourselves, as Paul advised the church in Corinth (1 Corinthians 13:5-7). Anything in our lives or ministry that is not in alignment with the Word and will of God, we must choose to put an end to it all, so we can continue to serve Him with a pure heart. Whatever is not in alignment with the Word and will of God, is not like God. That's right, we must end what is not like GOD. JESUS already finished the work, and He sent the Holy Spirit so we would be empowered to do what we cannot do on our own. GOD is with you.

When your inside is pure, then what you show outwardly is simply a reflection of such; **look in.** Moreover, this is what we want to convey to those who hold us in high regard. We should share the sentiment of the apostle, Paul, when he said, "follow me as I follow Christ" (1

Corinthians 11:1).

As a leader, in examining yourself, is there anything in your heart that keeps it from being pure and in what ways can you recognize a pure heart in life and ministry?

PRAYER:

LORD, JESUS, forgive me for the times where I was more focused on religion and not relationship; for the times when ceremonial routines overrode me allowing Your Spirit to have full control. May I never be in the way of Your move, LORD; however You want to move. May I never be a stumbling block to others because of what I do religiously. While I understand the importance of praying religiously, reading Your Word religiously, serving You religiously, may I never forget and always be reminded that what I do religiously is only a reflection of an internal transformation You have done in me. Thank you, Holy Spirit, for reminding me that I have religion only because of my relationship with You, and not relationship because of religion! GOD, You are Great! "Search me, Oh God, and know my heart: try me, and know my thoughts: And see if there be any wicked way in me, and lead me in the way everlasting..." (Psalm 139:23-24). LORD...

Day Eleven

"Trust God"
Luke 12:22-32

Then He said to His disciples, "Therefore I say to you, do not worry about your life, what you will eat; nor about the body, what you will put on. ²³ Life is more than food, and the body is more than clothing. ²⁴ Consider the ravens, for they neither sow nor reap, which have neither storehouse nor barn; and God feeds them. Of how much more value are you than the birds? ²⁵ And which of you by worrying can add one cubit to his stature? ²⁶ If you then are not able to do the least, why are you anxious for the rest? ²⁷ Consider the lilies, how they grow: they neither toil nor spin; and yet I say to you, even Solomon in all his glory *was not arrayed like one of these.* [28] *If then God so clothes the grass, which today is in the field and tomorrow is thrown into the oven, how much more will He clothe you, O you of little faith?* [29] *"And do not seek what you should eat or what you should drink, nor have an anxious mind.* [30] *For all these things the nations of the world seek after, and your Father knows that you need these things.* [31] *But seek the kingdom of God, and all these things shall be added to you.* [32] *"Do not fear, little flock, for it is your Father's good pleasure to give you the kingdom (NKJV).*

Bills and more bills, the children, the marriage, the job, the family, the illness, the friends, the church, the community center, the membership (congregation), your personal health, etc. So many things concern us. Jesus told his disciples to not concern themselves with their cares – things they have no control over.

The coronavirus pandemic certainly put the lives of many in an uproar: deaths, financial difficulties, and for churches, a great scattering of congregations as we have been catapulted into virtual ministry. No pastor after God's heart, wants to see sheep scattered or the needs of the church go neglected. For some, during the COVID-19 pandemic, tithes and offering increased, for others it diminished, leaving the responsibility of the mortgage or lease to the pastor and/or the church staff.

Despite the unprecedented circumstances of our lives and ministries, Jesus knew. Jesus knows. As a servant-leader, our role in such circumstances is not to figure it all out, but to believe and trust God through it all. Being confident that He has worked it out.

We should never forget that it is our "Father's good pleasure to give us the Kingdom" (Luke 12:32). There is no lack or scattering in God's Kingdom – spiritually and naturally. So, **trust GOD.**

As a servant-leader, in what ways can you practice trusting God more in your life and ministry?

PRAYER: LORD, help me to maintain focus on You and what Your will is for me. My desire is to trust You more, walk in obedience to Your Word, and what You have given me to do. During those moments where distraction is strong and worry is heightened, I pray for Your guidance and strength to "seek Your Kingdom" understanding that everything I need, both natural and spiritual, according to Your will, will be added unto me (Luke 12:31). Lord, I know You know my heart, but I want to say thank You for being so good to me. I love You and I do not serve You for blessings and for my requests to be granted, but I love You and serve You because You love me; and You are good, and Your mercy endures forever. I love and serve You because Your faithfulness is a hook in my heart that pulls me closer to You daily. I am grateful to be called Yours and am grateful for the benefits that come with belonging to You. LORD...

Day Twelve

"A Faithful & Focused Servant "
Luke 12:41-48

Then Peter said to Him, "Lord, do You speak this parable only to us, or to all people?" ⁴² And the Lord said, "Who then is that faithful and wise steward, whom his master will make ruler over his household, to give them their portion of food in due season? ⁴³ Blessed is that servant whom his master will find so doing when he comes. ⁴⁴ Truly, I say to you that he will make him ruler over all that he has. ⁴⁵ But if that servant says in his heart, 'My master is delaying his coming,' and begins to beat the male and female servants, and to eat and drink and be drunk, ⁴⁶ the master of that servant will come on a day when *he is not looking for him, and at an hour when he is not aware, and will cut him in two and appoint him his portion with the unbelievers.* [47] *And that servant who knew his master's will and did not prepare himself or do according to his will, shall be beaten with many stripes.* [48] *But he who did not know, yet committed things deserving of stripes, shall be beaten with few. For everyone to whom much is given, from him much will be required; and to whom much has been committed, of him they will ask the more (NKJV).*

It is not enough to know what to do and how to do it, but it must be embedded in our hearts so that knowing what and how becomes an action in our lives. In other words, to teach the right lessons and how to apply it but not live or apply what we teach will not get us into Heaven nor will it have an impact on those we lead. GOD's Word, our faith, and lifestyle is what will help us succeed in our personal lives, our ministry, and our influence.

Some people are mean and cruel, as it is sometimes a reflection of their brokenness. That is why it is so important, as a servant-leader, to stay focused on what GOD has purposed us to do. The devotional Scripture points out "Who then is that faithful and wise steward, whom his master will make ruler over His household, to give them their portion of food in due season? Blessed is that servant whom his master will find so doing when He comes?" (Luke 12:42-43).

My fellow servant-leader, when we are focused on GOD and the assignment He has given us, we put ourselves in a position to allow God to show us where people are, so we can assess how we will interact with them (to help them, guide them, or give them space for a time); and not react in a manner that misrepresents Christ. We may not always be able to pinpoint their actual situation but being in tune with God enables us to identify their condition: sadness, brokenness, broken heart, anger, frustration, rejection, oppression, etc.

One of our leadership goals as a Christian must be to always evolve in GOD. That does not excuse our responsibility and accountability to others, but the more we grow in God, the more God entrusts us with assignments that we are able to complete and have an impact in the lives of the people He wants us to serve (help, guide, and equip).

Servant-leaders, certainly the goal is not more assignments, but to whom much is given, much is required; which is why we must remain **focused and faithful.** The more we serve GOD according to His will, the more He trusts us (not just us trusting Him). So here, His "more assignments" is a trust He has in us to make a greater impact. As we evolve in GOD, His Kingdom expands through us.

As a servant-leader, in what ways can you practice maintaining your focus on GOD and what He has entrusted you with to have an impact in your life and ministry?

PRAYER:

LORD, help me to maintain focus on You and what Your will is for me. My desire is to walk in obedience to Your Word. I will not complain about the tasks You have given me. It is an honor to be employed by You; to be chosen to be a life-changer for others. Restore my passion and zeal to serve You and people.

LORD JESUS, You are my reward and there is no greater blessing than You being my forever portion. And, LORD . . .

Day Thirteen

"Be Compassionate"
Luke 13:1-5

There were present at that season some who told Him about the Galileans whose blood Pilate had mingled with their sacrifices. ² And Jesus answered and said to them, "Do you suppose that these Galileans were worse sinners than all other Galileans, because they suffered such things? ³ I tell you, no; but unless you repent you will all likewise perish. ⁴ Or those eighteen on whom the tower in Siloam fell and killed them, do you think that they were worse sinners than all other men who dwelt in Jerusalem? ⁵ I tell you, no; but unless you repent you will all likewise perish." (NKJV)

Jesus clearly points out that bad experiences do not mean "deserved-experiences." You know the saying, or the question that is often asked, "Why do bad things happen to good people?" Well, this is what happens in life; to non-Christians and Christians. "Yes, and all who desire to live godly in Christ Jesus will suffer persecution" (2 Timothy 3:12, NKJV). The Message Bible of the same Scripture states, "Anyone who wants to live all out for Christ is in for a lot of trouble; there's no getting around it." Trouble comes to everyone, but it's how we go through it that determines both the outcome and our development. Furthermore, trouble comes to everyone despite how "good" or "bad" they are.

As a brief point of reference, in Job chapters 4 through 23, Job's friends accused him of having done something wrong in order to be as sick as he was. They accused him of sin. Many of us are not only able to identify with Job, but if we were to be honest, some of us have played Job's friends.

Oh, you know, that friend or family member who had a major weight loss; assumptions are made that he or she is sick or that they had some type of procedure to look that way. Accusations. Even if those thoughts were not said to the individual directly, accusations have been made. Such blame can play a part in hindering one's spiritual growth, or discouragement, or even fuel their frustrations, making matters worse; especially when we share our thoughts with others.

Herein lies the question, "Where's the compassion?" Even to the most difficult people; where's the compassion? When we look at the circumstances of others and determine that what they are experiencing is what they deserve, we are not operating in compassion. As servant-leaders, when we are sincerely concerned about the well-being of others, we cannot spend time focusing on their lifestyle to determine the reason for their troubles. Certainly, we do not condone sin, but here the focus is compassion. Jesus did not condone sin either, however, He did not lack in kind-heartedness. In fact, our concern should portray compassion; the compassion that Christ extended to the lowest and greatest of men and women.

A circumstance or two may have come to mind that you could say, "I may have misjudged, mishandled, misappropriated, or even misunderstood a person or situation. God, forgive me!" The apostle Paul said, "For by the grace given me I say to every one of you: Do not think of yourself more highly than you ought, but rather think of yourself with sober judgment, in accordance with the faith God has distributed to each of you" (Romans 12:3, NIV). To get my point across more directly, the New Living Translation states this verse of Scripture like this:

Because of the privilege and authority God has given me, I give each of you this warning: Don't think you are better than you really are. Be honest in your evaluation of yourselves, measuring yourselves by the faith God has given us" (Romans 12:3, NLT).

As time goes by, we can sometimes forget that we were once in the same predicament as those we talk about. It may not be the same exact situation, but we have had the same feelings; and we all had a desperate need for GOD's rescue at some point or many points in our lives. Paul had to remind the church in Corinth that they ought to be so mindful of their faith in Christ that they represent Him with their behavior and interaction with one another. He told them not to: judge and misjudge. We ought to have a clear understanding on how to appropriate judgment so we will know how to help. Paul said "It isn't my responsibility to judge outsiders, but it is certainly your responsibility to judge those inside the church who are sinning" (1 Corinthians 5:12, NLT). If we want to win souls, we must be wise not to judge. If we want to keep (nurture, preserve, and warn) souls, we must be wise to judge, yet restore with the "spirit of meekness" (Galatians 6:1). In other words, be gentle *(NIV, NKJV, NLT)*. So we want to ...

1. **Not allow the "world" to see all of our issues** and settle our disputes (1 Corinthians 6:1-8).

2. **Remember that we were not always saved** and not everyone comes from a church background (1 Corinthians 6:8-11). Therefore, a little compassion goes a long way!

3. **Be compassionate.** Extend to others the unconditional grace that Christ has extended to you. You may say, "Well, I'm not Christ, and I've been through too much for too long!" Very true, my fellow servant-leader. None of us are Jesus Christ, but if we claim He lives in our hearts and that He is

LORD of our lives, then the compassion we extend to others, no matter who they are or what they've done, is an extension of His unconditional grace. It is not an easy task, but it is a crucial one.

Again, in Luke 13, Jesus made it very clear that the tragedies that befell the Galileans at the hands of Pilate or the catastrophe of the fallen Siloam towers, which killed eighteen people, were not a result of some sin that those who died committed. However, He did say unless we repent of our sin, we will perish. So then what was Jesus' point? I'm glad you asked! Jesus is emphatically pointing out that just because none of those tragedies happened to you does not mean that you are exempt from repentance!

As a servant-leader, in what ways can you practice a deeper sense of compassion and repentance in your life and ministry?

PRAYER:

LORD, JESUS... forgive me. Forgive me for what I have said about others that was ungodly, forgive me for what I thought about others that was ungodly, forgive me for judging and misjudging others, forgive me for not displaying the compassion You've so graciously given to me, and forgive me for misrepresenting You in the process. Forgive me, LORD. Thank you for reminding me that I am not exempt from repentance. As I take a spiritual evaluation of myself, LORD, ever reveal myself to me, especially the things that need to change (even those things I don't recognize), so that I may repent of my wrongdoings, be conformed to Your ways, and be the example You want me to be. LORD…

Day Fourteen

"Count Up The Cost"
Luke 14:25-35

Now great multitudes went with Him. And He turned and said to them, ²⁶ "If anyone comes to Me and does not hate his father and mother, wife and children, brothers and sisters, yes, and his own life also, he cannot be My disciple. ²⁷ And whoever does not bear his cross and come after Me cannot be My disciple. ²⁸ For which of you, intending to build a tower, does not sit down first and count the cost, whether he has enough to finish it — ²⁹ lest, after he has laid the foundation, and is not able to finish, all who see it begin to mock him, ³⁰ saying, 'This man began to build and was not able to finish?'

³¹ Or what king, going to make war against another king, does not sit down first and consider whether he is able with 10,000 to meet him who comes against him with 20,000? ³² Or else, while the other is still a great way off, he sends a delegation and asks conditions of peace. ³³ So likewise, whoever of you does not forsake all that he has cannot be My disciple. ³⁴ 'Salt is good; but if the salt has lost its flavor, how shall it be seasoned?' ³⁵ It is neither fit for the land nor for the dunghill, but men throw it out. He who has ears to hear, let him hear!" (NKJV)

That'll be $250.83" is what the cashier told me at the supermarket when I went there with the intention of picking up far less than what I purchased. I had $100 to $125 in mind for spending, not $250! The truth of the matter is, I did not count up the cost. I went to the supermarket hungry, and everything that looked good to me went into that cart! When the cashier said $250.83, I had a decision to make about something that I did not calculate. I did not count up the cost. In that moment, I had to decide if I was going to either put some items back, pay for the entire bill as it was, or walk out of the store without anything at all.

In this devotional Scripture Jesus gave what seemed

to be a tough ultimatum. "Forsake it all or no Me at all" pretty much sums it up. Jesus wasn't really endorsing hate or separation as much as He was placing emphasis on three things:

1. He comes before all things in our life.

2. Self-sacrifice.

3. There's no room for a life of sin (the way of the world) and Him; pick one.

Jesus was being emphatically clear that we cannot value anything or anyone, including ourselves, more than Him. Servant-leaders, remember when you first received Jesus as Lord of your life? It was a life-changing moment to know that the Savior lives in your heart and is Lord of your life. We felt safe, secure, and assured. Until that first big trial or tribulation came that interrupted our "honeymoon phase" of being a Christian. Like my supermarket experience, it's because we did not count up the cost of what it means to live for Christ.

Serving the Lord comes with disappointments, heartbreaks, loss of friendships, and many transformative ex-

THE *Servant Leader's Devotional*

periences. Our transformation is constant because the aim is to be like JESUS, no matter the cost. The determination we must make is that everything you've experienced up to this point is all worth it for the cause of Christ.

As I looked into that grocery cart, I put back some things I did not need; things that were not good for me, and things that were not really necessary. You see, "all things are lawful, but not all things are expedient" (1 Corinthians 10:23). While we are allowed to make our own decisions, we have to count up the cost of whatever we decide on. This includes not holding on to people and things that are not beneficial to your personal development, the example you are, and influence you have on people.

My grocery bill did not lessen significantly, but the test is in knowing what I did not need and having the willingness to pay for what I did need. Our relationship with Christ and the call of God on our life comes with great sacrifice on our part and a willingness to submit to the will of God. **We pay the price because serving Him is worth the cost.**

As a servant-leader, in what ways can you count up the cost better in your life and ministry? What do you need to remove? What do you need to take on?

PRAYER:

LORD, forgive me for not adding up the cost and for trying to do things my way which only disrupted my peace and delayed my process. I see now, LORD, that I have not been waiting on You, but You've been waiting for me to completely yield to Your plan. There were some things I didn't want to let go of, not realizing that "letting go" is the cost to having You. GOD, you know all things, but I will still be fully transparent with You. I need You, LORD and ...

Day Fifteen

"Lost in the House"
Luke 15:11-32

T hen He said: "A certain man had two sons. ¹²
And the younger of them said to his father,
'Father, give me the portion of goods that falls
to me.' So he divided to them his livelihood. ¹³
And not many days after, the younger son gathered all together, journeyed to a far country, and there wasted his possessions
with prodigal living. ¹⁴ But when he had spent all, there arose a
severe famine in that land, and he began to be in want. ¹⁵ Then
he went and joined himself to a citizen of that country, and he
sent him into his fields to feed swine. ¹⁶ And he would gladly
have filled his stomach with the pods that the swine ate, and no

one gave him anything. [17] *But when he came to himself, he said, 'How many of my father's hired servants have bread enough and to spare, and I perish with hunger!* [18] *I will arise and go to my father, and will say to him, "Father, I have sinned against heaven and before you,* [19] *and I am no longer worthy to be called your son. Make me like one of your hired servants."* [20] *And he arose and came to his father. But when he was still a great way off, his father saw him and had compassion, and ran and fell on his neck and kissed him.* [21] *And the son said to him, 'Father, I have sinned against heaven and in your sight, and am no longer worthy to be called your son.'* [22] *But the father said to his servants, 'Bring out the best robe and put it on him, and put a ring on his hand and sandals on his feet.* [23] *And bring the fatted calf here and kill it, and let us eat and be merry;* [24] *for this my son was dead and is alive again; he was lost and is found.' And they began to be merry.* [25] *Now his older son was in the field. And as he came and drew near to the house, he heard music and dancing.* [26] *So he called one of the servants and asked what these things meant.* [27] *And he said to him, 'Your brother has come, and because he has received him safe and sound, your father has killed the fatted calf.'* [28] *But he was angry and would not go in. Therefore, his father came out and pleaded with him.* [29] *So he answered and said to his father, 'Lo, these many years I have been serving you; I never transgressed your commandment at any time; and yet you never gave me a young goat, that I might make merry with my friends.* [30] *But as soon as this son of yours came, who has devoured your livelihood with harlots, you killed the fatted calf for him.'* [31] *And he said to him, 'Son, you are always with me, and all that I have is yours.* [32] *It was right that we should make merry and be glad, for your brother was dead and is alive again, and was lost and is found.'"* (NKJV)

If we seek to be celebrated, we miss out on the opportunity to encourage and celebrate others.

I know the story all too well; you toil day and night. You work hard. You fast and pray consistently. What God says do, you do, but it seems that the wayward get more rewarded, and you continue to struggle as you wait on GOD.

The challenge and reflection here is to see beyond the visual reality of your situation. God built and continues to build your character and integrity during your waiting period. During the times that you feel unappreciated and devalued, remain consistent.

The prodigal son's brother felt unappreciated and unrecognized for all he did. We can say that while his little brother, known as the prodigal son, was lost (because he intentionally strayed from home, only to find that the world had nothing for him), that this older brother was lost as well. Lost in the house. Have you ever been "lost in the house?" Serving the LORD and people can really take a toll on you. As mentioned in the previous devotions, long hours of counseling, praying, even studying, and preparing sermons, visiting the sick, visiting prisons, officiating weddings, doing eulogies, marital obligations, and family obligations; the list can go on, can wear you out. Yet, you may feel like no one takes into account all you do. From your family to your church family to your friends, and even to your boss or colleagues. It can be unsettling to see others celebrated when they have not done half of what you have labored in; both naturally and spiritually. It can make you want to give up or not do anything for anyone anymore, but that's how we get lost in the house.

With feelings of inadequacy such as feeling unappreciated, the question then is, "Who are you doing all of it for?" It should be a convicting question that should provoke us to "pursue peace." When we have peace, we can labor without complaining and without needing validation. While many of us may not like that word, at the end of day, if you feel unappreciated to the degree that you don't want to celebrate what GOD is doing for someone else or feel like you deserve it over them, you are looking for validation. However, the Father has already validated you by enabling you to do all you do; and there is no work you do that will go unrewarded by God, naturally and spiritually.

No matter how you give, be it your time, monetarily, or any other way that you give of yourself, remember it is all to the glory of GOD. The older son gave so much and was so upset about feeling devalued that when there was a celebration for the return of his little brother, the prodigal son, he didn't show up to the welcome home party. The father noticed his oldest son was missing from the celebration. So, the father went to get him!

That's what God does for us. He will always come get us to let us know that we are not excluded from His plan. When we go into our shell or have a pity party, we must remind ourselves that God is our reward, and that God is enough. In His faithfulness, GOD will always remind us that everything He has, we have, because we are His.

"By His divine power, God has given us everything we need for living a godly life. We have received all of this by coming to know Him, the One who called us to Himself by means of His marvelous glory and excellence. And because of His glory and excellence, He has given us great and precious promises. These are the promises that enable you to share His divine nature and escape the world's corruption caused by human desires. In view of all of this, make every effort to respond to God's promises. Supplement your faith with generous provision of moral excellence, and moral excellence with knowledge, and knowledge with self-control, and self-control with patient endurance, and patient endurance with godliness, and godliness with brotherly affection, and brotherly affection with love for everyone" (2 Peter 1:3-7, NLT)."

Servant-leader, you are too valuable to GOD to be lost in the House. Cherish your worth.

As a servant-leader, in what ways can you practice remembering your value to God and remember God's promise for your life and ministry?

PRAYER:

Father, GOD, in the Name of JESUS, do not let me be "lost in the house." I don't want to serve you and yet be lost; praise you and help others; and yet be lost. I don't want to preach the Gospel and yet be lost. Forgive me for the times when I felt I deserved more for the work that You have empowered and graced me to do. I value the anointing You have placed in my life. You complete me LORD and serving You in any capacity is an honor and a privilege. May I ever have your peace, compassion, and joy, that I do not serve begrudgingly. LORD, GOD...

Day Sixteen

"God's Word is Sufficient "
Luke 16:19-31

There was a certain rich man who was clothed in purple and fine linen and fared sumptuously every day. *20* But there was a certain beggar named Lazarus, full of sores, who was laid at his gate, *21* desiring to be fed with the crumbs which fell from the rich man's table. Moreover, the dogs came and licked his sores. *22* So it was that the beggar died and was carried by the angels to Abraham's bosom. The rich man also died and was buried. *23* And being in torments in Hades, he lifted up his eyes and saw Abraham afar off, and Lazarus in his bosom. *24* Then he cried and said, 'Father Abraham, have mercy on me, and send

Lazarus that he may dip the tip of his finger in water and cool my tongue; for I am tormented in this flame.' [25] *But Abraham said, 'Son, remember that in your lifetime you received your good things, and likewise Lazarus evil things; but now he is comforted, and you are tormented.* [26] *And besides all this, between us and you there is a great gulf fixed, so that those who want to pass from here to you cannot, nor can those from there pass to us.'* [27] *Then he said, 'I beg you therefore, father, that you would send him to my father's house,* [28] *for I have five brothers, that he may testify to them, lest they also come to this place of torment.'* [29] *Abraham said to him, 'They have Moses and the prophets; let them hear them.'* [30] *And he said, 'No, father Abraham; but if one goes to them from the dead, they will repent.'* [31] *But he said to him, 'If they do not hear Moses and the prophets, neither will they be persuaded though one risen from the dead'"* (NKJV).

Jesus tells the story of the rich man and Lazarus. He tells of how Lazarus was a poor and sickly beggar, while the rich man was consumed by his possessions and did not help those in need. Both men die. Lazarus goes to heaven, and the rich man goes to hell.

Jesus was not painting a picture that to be poor is good

and righteous and to be rich is evil and full of sin. Indeed, there are poor people who will go to hell, and rich people who will go to heaven. Here, in this devotional Scripture, Jesus is addressing the heart. The intent of the heart. God searches the hearts of mankind (Jeremiah 17:10; Psalms 139:23-24; Romans 8:27).

This devotional is also about believing God's Word! The rich man wanted Abraham to send Lazarus as resurrected proof so that his family may be saved from the torment of hell. Jesus concludes this story by saying that if the Word of the Lord spoken by the prophets was not sufficient enough for them to believe, neither will one's resurrection from the dead be believed. Your faith is based on believing what God said, not only by what He did!

What God did and does constantly proves our need to rely on His Word. It even boosts our confidence and trust in Him. John 1:1 states, "In the beginning was the Word, and the Word was with God and the Word was God..." Everything began with God's Word, and Jesus is the WORD (John 1:14; Revelation 19:13). Miracle, signs, and wonders will occur as GOD uses us for such, but it is the Word of God that transforms.

After He resurrected, Jesus said to Thomas "… because you have seen Me, you have believed. Blessed are those who have not seen and yet have believed" (John 20:29, NKJV). God's Word is sufficient. The Word of God is indeed enough to elevate our faith, to carry and strengthen us during trying times, and to anticipate the manifestation of His promises.

While God's Word is sufficient, it is our responsibility and charge to believe that Word; and convey this Truth we believe to others, so they, too, will believe (Luke 22:32).

GOD's Word and the promises of His Word are enough! Believe that!

As a servant-leader, in what ways can you practice believing God's Word more for your life, relationship(s), and ministry?

PRAYER:

LORD, witnessing what You have done in my life throughout the years is not only a blessing, but Father, it is a miracle. The way You have kept me and provided for my family and me, I stand in awe of You and am convinced that everything You've said in Your Word about You is true, and what You've said in Your Word about me is true. I not only believe in You, GOD. I believe You. LORD…

Day Seventeen

"Let Go - Let God"
Luke 17:3-4; 23:34-43

Take heed to yourselves. If your brother sins against you, rebuke him; and if he repents, forgive him. ⁴ And if he sins against you seven times in a day, and seven times in a day returns to you, saying, 'I repent,' you shall forgive him" (NKJV).

³⁴ Then Jesus said, "Father, forgive them, for they do not know what they do." And they divided His garments and cast lots. ³⁵ And the people stood looking on. But even the rulers with them sneered, saying, "He saved others; let Him save Himself if He is the Christ, the chosen of God." ³⁶ The soldiers

also mocked Him, coming and offering Him sour wine, [37] *and saying, "If You are the King of the Jews, save Yourself."* [38] *And an inscription also was written over Him in letters of Greek, Latin, and Hebrew: THIS IS THE KING OF THE JEWS.* [39] *Then one of the criminals who were hanged blasphemed Him, saying, "If You are the Christ, save Yourself and us."* [40] *But the other, answering, rebuked him, saying, "Do you not even fear God, seeing you are under the same condemnation?* [41] *And we indeed justly, for we receive the due reward of our deeds; but this Man has done nothing wrong."* [42] *Then he said to Jesus, "Lord, remember me when You come into Your kingdom."* [43] *And Jesus said to him, "Assuredly, I say to you, today you will be with Me in Paradise" (NKJV).*

After being beaten until He was unidentifiable, Jesus was crucified. He was nailed to a cross and berated by many who stood by, including one of the thieves that was being crucified next to him. Yet, in agony and what seemed like a moment of despair, Jesus said "Father forgive them for they know not what they do" (Luke 23:34). Jesus understood that His purpose was greater than His adversity and persecution. So, Jesus' act of forgiveness was displayed in His willingness to fulfill the will of the Father by laying down His life, so we can have life.

Many of us have experienced some major blows in our lives that make it more than difficult to forgive; to let go and let God. The difficulty to forgive can stem from:

1. The trauma and/or depth of the offense or

2. The fact that the offenses are ongoing. It is hard to forgive something that keeps happening or someone that keeps offending.

As servant-leaders, we often build relationships with other leaders. They become our comrade, our confidante, our spiritual brother or sister, our friend; and some our mentee or mentor. For some reason or another, divisiveness or derision may have arose in such relationships and has really put a dent in our hearts. Many don't realize or understand how deep a betrayal wound is. When someone you once trusted is no longer trustworthy, we have to continue to teach, sing, prophesy, preach, etc., while dealing with the turmoil of brokenness; until we are healed. It's during these times that God shows us that we need to trust His ability to heal us as we forgive. We must also trust God to place trustworthy people in our lives.

People don't always understand that when you have

someone preaching in your stead on a Sunday morning, or the worship leader has one of the worship team members leading praise and worship in their stead on a Sunday morning, it is sometimes because we are taking time to heal from what we have been inflicted with. As servant-leaders, the role that we have, the accountability we are entrusted with for those who follow and trust our leadership does not change because we've been hurt or betrayed by someone we've trusted. However, those are the moments in our Christian walk that we, as servant-leaders have an opportunity to become or remain diligent and committed. "Be steadfast, unmovable, always abounding in the work of the Lord, knowing that your labor is not in vain in the Lord" (1 Corinthians 15:58). Furthermore, this is an exemplary portrayal of being consistent; instant in and out of season (2 Timothy 4:2).

Certainly, we should never deny when we are hurting; that's how we get to the root of issues so we can be healed. However, we must also recognize that the kingdom picture is much larger than our situation. God told Ezekiel to not mourn his wife and to grieve quietly. When he was questioned, Ezekiel said he was obeying God because he was being used as an example of God's message to the Jews in that particular text (Ezekiel 24:15-27). Now, if we did not know God, it can sound a bit uncaring of God to tell Ezekiel not to mourn his wife, but the truth of the matter is there was a Message from God to the people in what He instructed Ezekiel to do; because HE cares.

I would go further to submit to you that through his obedience, Ezekiel found comfort in obeying God by doing what He was purposed to do; prophesy. So, what am I saying? God over everything! You can hurt, but you'll find comfort and healing in your obedience to God in fulfilling what you have been purposed to do. Sometimes healing happens when we are serving. Let go - let God.

For some, the repeated assaults (be it physical, spiritual, emotional, or mental) are too great to move on from. Is it worth separating you from God? Is it worth losing your anointing to bitterness and unforgiveness? Is it worth robbing others of being blessed by your ministry? Let me answer that for you. Nothing is worth losing your anointing. Nothing is worth sacrificing the great impact God purposes for you to have in the lives of others; nothing should separate you from the love of GOD (romans 8:39). Forgive them and LET IT GO! "If you do not forgive others their trespasses, neither will your Father forgive your trespasses" (Matthew 6:15, ESV).

Servant-leader, be reminded that you are included in that forgiveness. Were you the offender, and you can't seem to grow past your mistakes so feel stuck? Forgive. Forgive yourself. Don't repeat the offensive pattern and LET IT GO! And when you receive God's forgiveness and forgive yourself, please don't behave as though what was done never happened; be prepared to boldly face the past if it will help the offended heal. Selah.

In the first few verses of Luke 17, Jesus taught to avoid occasions of offense; either as the offender or the offended. However, He taught that while we may attempt to avoid occasions of offense, offenses will still come, so what do we do in those circumstances? Jesus said, "Forgive!"

No matter how many times you get offended, continue to forgive. You may never get the apology you're looking for. GOD is making you through it. He is making you more like Him. He is making sure that your influence is positive, and your impact is transforming. We must remember, it is not about us, it is about JESUS and the plan of GOD for our lives and our ministries.

One of the thieves on the cross chose to not repent for his sins and to join in with the others who antagonized Jesus, but it did not make Jesus come down from the Cross! HE died and resurrected for all humanity - this included those who offended Him and rejected Him; and those who continue to offend and reject Him today. The point is that although you may never receive the apology you're looking for or the apology you deserve. God is continually making you like Him as He brings you through it. So, choose to forgive. The Lord is making sure your influence is effective and your impact is transforming. We must remember it is not about us. It is about JESUS, the plan of GOD for our lives and our ministries, and to be a blessing to others.

Sometimes GOD will lead you, as the offended to ask the offender to forgive you. All the while, you are actually saying in your heart, "I forgive you." This is the power of forgiveness. Acts of forgiveness such as this can and will release you to places far beyond your desire or imagination.

Let go – Let GOD.

As a servant-leader, in what ways can you practice forgive-

ness in your life and ministry?

PRAYER:

My GOD, My Father; My GOD, My Father. Forgive me again. Just when I thought I was over something, something else occurred that peeled the band-aid off of my scar too soon. LORD, while I know that both healing and forgiveness is a choice I have to make, I realize that healing cannot begin until forgiveness is complete. Help me to release what is causing me pain so Your healing can begin. I'll be honest, GOD, I just cannot do this without You. HELP ME, LORD. HELP. Holy Spirit, saturate my heart and my mind. Grant me the peace that surpasses my understanding so that I can, with Your grace and peace, forgive. Do not allow my heart and my thoughts to be interrupted by pain and confusion. Thank you for the power to silence the noise that comes from the inner-me and the enemy; Satan, the LORD rebuke you in the Name of JESUS; the BLOOD OF JESUS is against you. GOD, root out, by the power of Your living Word and Your Holy Spirit, everything that is associated with any unforgiveness in my heart; take away the uneasiness. Create in me, oh God, a clean heart and renew the right spirit within me. Thank you, Jesus, for never letting me go, never giving up on me, and healing me from the inside-out. LORD...

Day Eighteen

"Continue to Pray"
Luke 18:1-8

Then He spoke a parable to them that men always ought to pray and not lose heart, ² saying: "There was in a certain city a judge who did not fear God nor regard man. ³ Now there was a widow in that city; and she came to him, saying, 'Get justice for me from my adversary.' ⁴ And he would not for a while; but afterward he said within himself, 'Though I do not fear God nor regard man, ⁵ yet because this widow troubles me I will avenge her, lest by her continual coming she weary me.'" ⁶ Then the Lord said, "Hear what the unjust judge said. ⁷ And shall God not avenge His own elect who cry out day and night to Him, though He bears long with them? [8] I tell you that He will avenge them speedily. Nevertheless, when the Son of Man comes, will He really find faith on the earth?" (NKJV).

"The grass is always greener on the other side." This famous saying goes back to the days of the poet Ovid (Publius Ovidius Naso, 43 B.C. - 17 A. D.); and likely before his time. Ovid wrote the proverb "harvest is always more fruitful in another man's fields." The metaphor, or figure of speech, is stating that the other side is not close by, so we really don't know what the grass looks like on the other side. Some of us have attempted to get to the other side; the other side being other people's statuses, relationships, or lifestyles. However, we soon learn that "the other side" isn't all it appeared to be from afar. Jesus' parable of the unjust judge not only gives light to how we ought to be importune (persistent) in prayer, but also gives revelation that the unjust judge had authority!

Do you realize how much authority and power you have when you pray and study God's Word?! Praying the Word of God is something every believer should put to practice and maintain. The Lord said, "so shall my Word be that goeth forth out of my mouth: it shall not return unto me void, but it shall accomplish that which I please, and it shall prosper in the thing whereto I sent it" (Isaiah 55:11, KJV).

When we consistently pray God's Word, something is bound to happen: miracles, answered petitions such as healing and change (transformation), not just of others, but of ourselves. Prayer transforms us too! When we are prayerful, we are not searching beyond God's provisions. Searching for greener grass of a place we can only see from a distance not only shows dissatisfaction and un-gratefulness on our part, but it is a rejection of the process of blessings that GOD has for us. The more we pray and study the Word of God, the more we pray God's Word. The more we pray God's Word, the more satisfied in JE-SUS we are. The more satisfied in Jesus we are, the more we become like Jesus. The more we become more like Jesus, the more we are concerned about the things that concern HIM.

Servant-leader, be steadfast and unmovable in your prayer time. You may not be able to pray for an hour or more every day, but you can pray consistently, every day; throughout the day, wherever you are!

Pray consistently. God will and God has answered. Get ready for expansion!

As a servant-leader, in what ways can you practice a deeper and more consistent prayer time in your life, relationships, and ministry?

PRAYER:

Dear LORD, give me a praying spirit. I not only ask for a praying spirit, but Holy Spirit, fill me and refill me. Restore my contentment with You, and the process You have me in. Give and restore my heavenly language that I may pray in the Spirit, because I know that even if I cannot interpret the tongues I speak, Holy Spirit, You know exactly what I am saying. Father, I pray for everyone and everything connected to me, from my immediate household to the stranger I get the opportunity to meet and tell about JESUS. Father, I pray for increase and overflow. I pray that You increase my concern for Your concerns. I pray for the United States of America, and all nations of the earth; cover and protect in the Name of Jesus. Father, the earth is Yours and everything in it.

I pray that You give me strength in the middle of the

night to stay awake to seek You. In advance, in the Name of Jesus, I rebuke Satan and his demons that come to cast spells on me and all God's people to keep us asleep; so that we are not on our praying post while demons run rampant in the earth. The Blood of Jesus. I pray now God, that You increase my hunger and desire for You; for they that hunger and thirst after Your righteousness shall be filled... fill me up, oh God, and let my cup overflow. An overflow of Your goodness, an overflow of Your mercy, an overflow of Your grace, an overflow of Your forgiveness, and overflow of Your healing, an overflow of Your joy, an overflow of Your peace, an overflow of Your strength, an overflow of Your anointing... overflow God. Exceedingly abundant above all I can ever ask or think according to Your power that is at work in me, overflow, I PRAY IN THE NAME OF JESUS. And LORD...

Day Nineteen

"The Blessings of Zacchaeus: Embrace Your *Next*"
Luke 19:1-10

Then Jesus entered and passed through Jericho. [2] Now behold, there was a man named Zacchaeus who was a chief tax collector, and he was rich. [3] And he sought to see who Jesus was but could not because of the crowd, for he was of short stature. [4] So he ran ahead and climbed up into a sycamore tree to see Him, for He was going to pass that way. [5] And when Jesus came to the place, He looked up and saw him, and said to him, "Zacchaeus, make haste and come down, for today I must stay at your house." [6] So he made haste and came down and received Him joyfully. [7] But when they saw it, they all complained, say-

ing, "He has gone to be a guest with a man who is a sinner." [8]
Then Zacchaeus stood and said to the Lord, "Look, Lord, I give
half of my goods to the poor; and if I have taken anything from
anyone by false accusation, I restore fourfold." [9] *And Jesus said*
to him, "Today salvation has come to this house, because he also
is a son of Abraham; [10] *for the Son of Man has come to seek and*
to save that which was lost." (NKJV)

Do you remember your "B.C." days; your Before
Christ days? The days before you received Jesus as Lord
of your life? I do. I remember how I enjoyed sin yet felt a
void that no sin or person could satisfy. Oh yes, I remember. In fact, I even remember my early years as a Christian. When people saw me, they saw a sinner. They did
not see a "sinner saved by grace" or a "new creature in
Christ" (Ephesians 2:5, 8; 2 Corinthians 5:17). The stigma
of my past was still on me, but God was transforming me
all the while.

Well, all who were around when Jesus called him by
name didn't see what Jesus saw. They saw Jesus call a
man, whose sin was publicly known, by name! Zacchaeus! Jesus saw a transformed man, a new man. Everyone
else saw old Zacchaeus, not realizing his present experi-

ence with Jesus was about to alter his future for the better and make his sin both the past and a testimony.

Servant-leader, once again, we must be careful not to deal with people based on the wrong they have done, or who or what they used to be. We all had a moment when the LORD called our name and we looked as unworthy as Zacchaeus. Paul reminded the church in Galatians 6:1-5:

> [1] Brethren, if a man be overtaken in a fault, ye which are spiritual, restore such one in the spirit of meekness; considering thyself, lest thou also be tempted. [2] Bear ye one another's burdens, and so fulfil the law of Christ. [3] For if a man think himself to be something, when he is nothing, he deceiveth himself. [4] But let every man prove his own work, and then shall he have rejoicing in himself alone, and not in another. [5] For every man shall bear his own burden. (KJV)

> [1] Dear brothers and sisters, if another believer is overcome by some sin, you who are godly should gently and humbly help that person back onto the right path. And be care-

ful not to fall into the same temptation your-self. [2] Share each other's burdens, and in this way obey the law of Christ. [3] If you think you are too important to help someone, you are only fooling yourself. You are not that import-ant. [4] Pay careful attention to your own work, for then you will get the satisfaction of a job well done, and you won't need to compare yourself to anyone else. [5] For we are each re-sponsible for our own conduct. (NLT)

Let's embrace all who come into the knowledge of Christ, because we don't want to deprive them of their next – wherever or whatever God intends for them.

Servant-leaders must be equally cautious not to dis-count ourselves. As time goes by, we can sometimes be-come complacent in how we serve and deem ourselves unfit for the change or elevation the Lord is presenting. We see a younger and possibly more innovative genera-tion behind us, and if we are honest, it can be intimidat-ing if we allow it. Be reminded that God needs you and what He has given you. He has equipped you for every phase in your life and ministry. So, be very careful not to discount yourself from your next!

If the Lord is calling your name to what's next for you, be readily available and confident to say, "Yes, LORD" with joy. Just like we preach and teach, "God is not through with you," there is still more He wants to get out of you. This is why He is yet calling you to do more.

May Jesus ever call you by your name, no matter where you are, and abide in your home, your heart, and your church, daily and always. May you ever be ready, with joy like Zacchaeus, to **embrace your next.** May **the blessing of Zacchaeus** be your portion always.

As a servant-leader, in what ways can you practice receiving the blessing of Zacchaeus in your life and ministry?

PRAYER:

LORD, thank you for knowing my name and calling me by name. Before I was in my mother's womb, Father, You knew me. Thank You for never counting me as a lost cause before I ever truly knew You. You are so amazing, GOD. You looked past my faults and said, "that one over there needs Me, let Me come to the rescue;" and without fail, GOD, You have rescued my life. May I never count others out, as I ever remember what You have done for me. Thank You that my past is not my present; and that any obstacles I face in the present is an opportunity to go through the right(eous) way, so that I can see the victory I am destined for. GOD...

Day Twenty

"Unrestricted Praise"
Luke 19:40

But He answered and said to them, "I tell you that if these should keep silent, the stones would immediately cry out" (NKJV).

While those around saw Jesus entering Jerusalem on a colt (a donkey), they praised God. Coming in on a donkey, traditionally, was a symbol of peace. Entering Jerusalem on a donkey portrayed Christ's humility.

While Jesus' entry into Jerusalem on a donkey is known as the "Triumphal Entry," others believe that it was an entry of disruption and judgment, as Jesus spoke words of destruction *and turned over tables of money changers at the temple (Luke 19:41-46).*

The Pharisees wanted the people quiet, but Jesus answered, "They can't be quiet." Why? Because God requires praise. After making that statement, Jesus wept; He lamented over Jerusalem. In his article Parousia Jesus, A Triumphal Entry, and the Fate of Jerusalem, Brent Kinman wrote, "After Jesus is greeted outside Jerusalem, the tenor of the episode turns quickly from joy to lament." To not acknowledge GOD with reverence is to grieve Him (Genesis 6:6; Psalm 78:40; Ephesians 4:30). How long will we ignore God's hands on our lives? How long will we overlook His presence? Just because GOD has not presented Himself in the way we had hoped or anticipated does not mean that He has not presented Himself.

You heard the saying, "we must trust God even when we can't trace Him." Being mindful and assured that GOD is always there should be the encouragement we need to praise Him without any restriction. Many don't realize that the servant-leader's praise can be restricted by the stresses of the responsibilities of the church; heat, heating system, air conditioning, water leaks, roofing

problems, the need for acoustics, renovations, life's tragedies, personal issues and trials, etc. The list goes on. Servant-leader, the challenge here is to put to action Psalm
34:1, to "bless the Lord at all times;" in our brightest and
darkest times.

One of the best things to see in a worship service is the
pastor and other church leaders participating in praise
and worship. Mike Passaro, one of the worship leaders
at The Summit Church in North Carolina said, "In many
ways, the pastor of the church controls the thermostat in
worship. The pastor's engagement in corporate singing
speaks to its value — both to the church and to the worship leader. A pastor that sings from the front row leads
his people by example. This time of singing matters. This
time of singing helps me believe the gospel. This time
of singing helps me sing the Word of God deep into my
heart and into the hearts of God's people."

Servant-leader, it is necessary to make a conscious de-
cision to publicly receive and worship our risen savior,
the Messiah, with the same humility He entered the earth
with. He lived, He ministered to all who would receive
Him, He entered Jerusalem on a donkey, and He died on

the Cross with humility! God wants you to receive Him in such a way that even amid the things you do not understand, you will always praise Him; with **unrestricted praise;** leading by example and setting the temperature for corporate worship and corporate blessings!

As a servant-leader, in what ways can you practice unrestricted praise in your life and ministry?

PRAYER:

LORD, I will not let anyone, anything, or any circumstance restrict my praise. I realize now that challenges are perfect opportunities to praise You through everything. Even when I can't feel You, or even when I don't hear You right away, I will always praise You right away! While my praise should be a public example, I will ever praise You; publicly and privately, because I love You and You are worthy. LORD…

Day Twenty One

"The Lord Has Need of You"
Luke 19:31-34; 24:49

And if anyone asks you, 'Why are you loosing it?' thus you shall say to him, 'Because the Lord has need of it.' ³² So those who were sent went their way and found it just as He had said to them. ³³ But as they were loosing the colt, the owners of it said to them, 'Why are you loosing the colt?' ³⁴ And they said, 'The Lord has need of him'" (NKJV).

⁴⁹ "Behold, I send the Promise of My Father upon you; but tarry in the city of Jerusalem until you are endued with power from on high" (NKJV).

Before Jesus' entry into Jerusalem on a colt (donkey), He gave instructions to His disciples to locate the colt; to loose it because "The Lord has need of him."

LIFE. Life has presented some scenarios and situations that can thwart us from purpose, if we allow it. Not that what we are doing doesn't serve a good cause, but sometimes weariness and displeasure creeps in because the "good" we are doing is not aligned with our God-ordained purpose.

It's a *good-work,* but is it a GOD-*work?*

Somehow, the busyness of life, family, work, and even ministry, pivoted our focus. Sometimes losing focus does not mean you've been distracted by negativity of some sort; but if the good you are doing still leaves you with a sense of dissatisfaction, it is time to re-evaluate what you are doing and seek the Lord for clear instructions. That dissatisfaction needs to be satisfied with purpose!

What was it that God has called you to? What business were you supposed to add to your ministry? What book were you supposed to write? What song or recording are you supposed to write and sing? What preaching series are you supposed record? Time is not so far gone that the Lord cannot use you for your purpose. The purpose which He designed specifically for you.

It doesn't matter that someone else may be doing something GOD has also called you to. Your purpose isn't defined by people, or by how many people are already doing it. It is given to you by God. The Lord has need of you, servant-leader!

Jesus has already been crucified and resurrected. He is not going to do it again. So, the power has been given to you. God is calling you to loose yourself! Untie yourself from whatever has you bound to what is not purposeful and embrace this journey God has designated for you.

They asked, "Why loose ye the colt?" (Luke 19:33), because "the Lord hath need of him" (Luke 19:34). The Lord has need of your gifts and talents, your ideas, your innovation, your testimonies, your **God-led transparency,** and the anointing He has placed in your life. He still has need of you; despite what you've done or been through. **The Lord has need of you!**

No more delays, no more setbacks, no more fear, your

portion is the Spirit of "power, love, and a sound mind" (2 Timothy 1:7). Now is the time to go forth. You have been graced with the power of the Holy Spirit to go forth!

As a servant-leader, in what ways can you practice recognizing your value to God and moving forward in your life and ministry?

PRAYER:

LORD, today I renounce fear and pride; and I embrace confidence in Your Word, and I embrace the confidence you have in me. I trust You Lord and place all my faith in You. Yet, my greatest joy is in knowing that the omnipotent and most gracious GOD has placed His trust in me. Thank You for trusting me to be a servant-leader for Your people, Lord. I accept Your trust and the assignments You entrust me with. LORD…

Made in the USA
Middletown, DE
30 March 2022